How to Give a Talk When You Don't Really Want To: Tips and Techniques to Improve Your Public Speaking

Michael D Callaghan

Published by Michael Callaghan, 2024.

While every precaution has been taken in the preparation of this book, the publisher assumes no responsibility for errors or omissions, or for damages resulting from the use of the information contained herein.

HOW TO GIVE A TALK WHEN YOU DON'T REALLY WANT TO: TIPS AND TECHNIQUES TO IMPROVE YOUR PUBLIC SPEAKING

First edition. June 9, 2024.

ISBN: 979-8224034376

Written by Michael D Callaghan.

Also by Michael D Callaghan

Angular Advocate
Developing Progressive Web Applications with Angular: How to Build and Deploy Mobile Applications without Paying Apple or Google for the Privilege

P-AI-R Programming
P-AI-R Programming: How AI Tools Like GitHub Copilot and ChatGPT Can Radically Transform Your Development Workflow
Pair Programming with Chat GPT

Standalone
Don't Say That at Work
Customizing ChatGPT: Quickly and Easily Create and Share Custom Business-Specific GPTs Without Code
How to Deploy Any Web Application to the Apple App Store
Sacrament Talk Mastery: How to Give a Sacrament Talk When You Really Don't Want To
The Scout Law of Leadership: 12 Attributes Every Leader (or Aspiring Leader) Should Cultivate
Techno Tales

¡No Digas Eso en el Trabajo! Lecciones que Puedes Usar para Mejorar tus Habilidades de Comunicación en los Negocios
How to Give a Talk When You Don't Really Want To: Tips and Techniques to Improve Your Public Speaking

Watch for more at https://walkingriver.com.

Table of Contents

How to Give a Talk When You Don't Really Want To

Tips and Techniques to Improve Your Public Speaking

Michael D. Callaghan

Abstract

In the professional world, effective communication and the ability to present information in a clear, organized, and engaging way is crucial. However, public speaking is often a daunting task for many. This comprehensive guide is designed to bolster your inherent communication skills and empower you to confidently articulate your ideas.

Is This Book for You?

Thank you for checking out this book.

Before we begin, let's spend a moment to decide whether this book is right for you. Do any of these sound like you?

- You get nervous about giving a public speech or presentation.

- You wonder whether anyone will want to hear what you have to say.

- Powerpoint presentations bore you to tears.

- You sometimes get tongue-tied and don't know what to say.

- You don't really know where to start when planning a presentation.

- Despite the above, you want to succeed.

This is a very short, straightforward book with useful and actionable tips you can employ right away. The techniques and suggestions come from my own personal and professional experience over three decades as a software developer and trainer.

I've made every mistake I warn about in the book. By including them, it is my hope that you can learn from my mistakes.

If that sounds good to you, then read on!

Introduction

Allow me to introduce you to the worst talk I have ever delivered (or seen delivered).

The Worst Talk Ever

Good morning, folks. [If no one responds, repeat it until you get a response.]

For those of you who don't know me, my name is Michael Callaghan and have been with this company for the past ten years.

Today I intend for my talk to be like a ghostly elevator – it will lift your spirits! [Chuckle at your own horrible joke]

My manager asked me to speak for a few minutes on the state of software development at our company. I don't know why she thought I was the right person to speak about this. I spent most of the week trying to get out of it, but I didn't do a very good job, so here I am. I hate speaking in public, even to small groups, so I put this off till this morning. I apologize in advance for this talk's poor quality. I was too bogged down with more important work to prepare.

Even so, I am grateful for the opportunity for me to get up to speak to you today. Talks are supposed to be a great opportunity for y'all to learn from me, but I definitely learned more writing it.

According to Wikipedia, the definition of software development is "the process of conceiving, specifying, designing, programming, documenting, testing, and bug fixing involved in creating and maintaining applications, frameworks, or other software components.", which is far better than the definition at dictionary.com. That site doesn't even attempt to define it.

To me, software development is a lot like those old Peanuts cartoons. For example, consider the Great Pumpkin. Linus proclaimed that "Halloween will soon be with us, and on Halloween night, the Great Pumpkin rises out of the pumpkin patch, and brings toys to all the good little children." The other characters in the cartoon react to Linus the same way many people in my family react when I talk about software.

I would like to share with you a story I heard at a conference once. Most of you are familiar with Alice in Lewis Carroll's classic novel Alice's Adventures in Wonderland. You will remember that she comes to a crossroads with two paths before her, each stretching onward but in opposite directions. As she contemplates which way to turn, she is confronted by the Cheshire Cat, of whom Alice asks, "Which path shall I follow?" The cat answers, "That depends where you want to go. If you do not know where you want to go, it doesn't matter which path you take." That, my friends, is how I feel some of our software projects go.

In conclusion, I'd like to thank you for coming.

I hope you experienced a few cringe-worthy moments while reading that. Throughout the rest of this book, I will explain why this was such a horrible talk, beyond its obvious problems, and provide you with a series of tips that will help make your next talk great – even if you don't want to give it!

Why Give a Talk

There are likely as many reasons to give a talk as there are to avoid it. However, that's not the point of this chapter. Here, I will outline the three primary types of talks you might be asked to give and discuss how they differ. The most effective talks often incorporate elements of all three to varying degrees.

Understanding the type of talk you're preparing for, and what should be included, can greatly simplify your presentation and enhance its impact.

To aid your memory, consider your talk as a PIE.

Persuasive

A persuasive talk aims to compel your audience to take action. Whether you're selling a product or service and want listeners to invest their money, or you're advocating for a new technology or process at work, these talks are challenging and necessitate thorough preparation.

It's crucial to recognize that your audience may be resistant to change. They are accustomed to the status quo and might see no reason to alter their perspective. The onus is on you to convince them and demonstrate the benefits of acting on your proposal.

You'll need a wealth of supporting evidence and examples from current or historical cases where similar changes have been successfully implemented.

Informative or Inspirational

Informative or inspirational talks don't necessarily prompt your audience to act on your behalf but rather provide information for their benefit.

You might also aim to inspire them to make changes in their own lives. While this could resemble a persuasive talk, the difference lies in your intent: you're not asking the audience to do something for you, but for themselves.

When crafting an informative or inspirational speech, remember that your goal is not to persuade but to inform or inspire your audience.

Your role is to supply information that they can apply to their lives or to encourage them to make positive changes for themselves.

Employing the word "you" more often than "I" can clarify your intent.

For example: "You can achieve anything if you believe in yourself" contrasts with "I believe in myself," and "You should work hard for what you want" differs from "I will work hard for what I want."

Avoid using the phrase "in my opinion." This can imply that your views are subjective and that there may be other valid opinions, which could suggest that you're delivering a persuasive speech—not your intention.

Entertaining

The primary objective of an entertaining talk is to amuse your audience. It's true that all talks should strive to avoid dullness, but entertainment should be tailored to the context.

While you should always aim to keep your audience engaged, there are settings where entertainment is inappropriate. For example, humor at a dinner party may be well-received, whereas a comedic approach at a funeral would likely be deemed unsuitable.

Most speeches can benefit from some form of entertainment, whether through humor or other means. Despite the gravity of a topic, lighthearted elements can make a talk more compelling. However, remember that not all presentations must be humorous; often, a serious demeanor can be just as, if not more, impactful.

Take, for instance, Steve Jobs' 2005 commencement address at Stanford University. He tackled profound themes of life and death, yet infused the speech with humor to provide levity:

> At 17, I encountered a saying that went something like: "If you live each day as if it were your last, eventually you will be correct." It left a mark on me, and for the past 33 years, I have asked myself every morning in the mirror: "If today were my last day, would I want to do what I'm about to do?" Whenever the answer has been "No" too many times in a row, I realize a change is necessary.

Your Content

If you've ever stood in front of a group and shared your knowledge, ideas, and insights with them, you know how nerve-wracking it can be. You want to ensure that your audience is captivated, engaged, and excited about what you have to say. After all, they may have traveled great lengths — both geographically and emotionally — to be in your presence.

When it comes to delivering a talk, people often feel overwhelmed. There are so many things to consider: What will the audience expect? How should I structure my content? Should I use visual aids or not? How should I pace myself? The list goes on and on. If you're ready to get serious about becoming an effective speaker who engages audiences like never before, read on.

What should you talk about?

How do you figure out what your presentation should be about? If someone asked you to deliver a talk, they probably gave you a topic already. From there, you may have lots of directions you can go. This is where it gets fun.

You can decide to give the talk in the form of a lecture. You might want to try something more creative. Instead of just giving a lecture, you could teach your audience a skill or give them an experience.

Maybe you have an idea for an event or a workshop. You could create something that will get people interacting with each other and learning together.

A final option is to do an activity with your audience. If you have time, and the setting is appropriate, you could lead them through a series of exercises that all have something to do with the topic of your talk.

You could even break into groups and assign them each one or two exercises to complete before they come back together again and share what they learned from their exercise(s). This is called "theatre games" in the world of theatre, which is pretty much exactly what it sounds like: people acting out scenes from their lives, working through problems together, being creative and having fun while exploring new perspectives on life's challenges.

By now you should be ready to start thinking about how you want your talk to be different from others that are already out there on the same topic. It's time for some brainstorming!

Brainstorming: How to make your talk unique

The first step in brainstorming is to give yourself some time to be creative. It doesn't have to take long, but you need to spend some time thinking about what you want your talk to be before you can figure out how you are going to do that.

Some of the ideas that will come up might seem crazy or impossible, but don't dismiss them too quickly. Often the most unexpected ideas are the best ones. Just remember that an idea may not work when it comes down to actually putting on a talk, so if one of your ideas seems like it would take too much time or money (or both) then don't worry about it! Keep brainstorming and don't allow yourself to get hung up on just one idea.

Here are some questions that can help you think of creative ways that your talk will be different from others out there on the same topic:

- What is something unusual or surprising about this topic?

- What have other people said about this topic? How could I do something completely different from what they did?

- How could I make my audience feel differently about this topic?

- How could I make my audience laugh or cry when they hear me speak?

- How could I make my audience feel like they are part of the experience with me?

- If I had no limits whatsoever, how would I put this talk together?

Once you have some ideas, select a couple, and see where they take you. Now it's time to take the next step.

How to organize your thoughts

How should you say it? How do you keep your audience engaged? How can you make sure that your presentation is as effective as possible?

It can be difficult to feel confident about how to do this, especially if you don't have a lot of experience. But it's not impossible and there are some simple steps that you can follow to give yourself the best chance at success. The first step is to understand the structure of a presentation.

A typical presentation usually begins with an introduction and ends with a conclusion. The introduction provides an overview of what will be covered in the talk. It also sets the tone for the content and lets your audience know what they can expect from your talk. It's important that this section is brief, interesting, and relevant so that people are drawn in right away. The conclusion should summarize what was covered during the talk and leave people feeling inspired or enlightened about what they just learned from you. This section typically includes a call-to-action that encourages people to act on what they just heard from you or use it as an opportunity for them to ask questions about anything else that was covered during your presentation.

The body of your talk is typically made up of three main parts: an opening statement or story, an explanation or description, and a summary or lesson learned from it all. An opening statement is used to grab attention immediately and set up whatever topic will be discussed during the talk. For example, if you're speaking to a group of business owners, you might begin with a story about how the success of your company was born from a problem you encountered. The explanation or description section delves into the details and is an opportunity for you to give more background about your topic. This is where you provide details about what exactly it is that you'll be talking about during your presentation. The summary or lesson learned from it all portion sums up everything that was covered throughout the talk and gives people an idea of what they can do with what they just heard from you.

The conclusion wraps up everything that was discussed in the body of your talk and is a great opportunity to leave the audience with something to think about. For example, if you're speaking on how to make a profit from an online business, you might want to leave your audience with the idea that they should take action and get started on their own online business now!

It's also important to remember that there are several other parts of a talk besides these main three. There may be times when you need to give special attention or ask questions of your audience. There may also be instances where you need to allow your audience time for questions or discussion. You may even want to include a story or quote at some point during your presentation. The most important thing is that you use these extra parts as needed, but don't overdo it and make your presentation too long by including too many extras just because they seem like good ideas at the time. Instead, keep it simple by sticking with the main parts of your talk and using any other parts sparingly as needed only when appropriate.

Visual Aids and Props

One question you need to answer early is whether you will be using visual aids or props in your talk. Will you be using PowerPoint or some other presentation software, or will it be more like a Ted Talk, where the audience's only focus is you? If you're not comfortable with technology, you may want to stick with a more traditional lecture style.

If you are going to use technology, the next step is deciding what types of visual aids or props to use. Will it be something physical? A diagram? A video clip? Will it be more abstract, like a metaphor or analogy?

As you're brainstorming, think about how your topic can be made visually interesting. For example, if you're discussing the future of education and how technology is changing the way we learn, show a video of someone using an online learning platform. If you're discussing the future of food and its sustainability, show photos or videos of people growing their own food or animal farms. If your topic is creativity in business, show examples of companies that are doing creative things in their marketing campaigns. These are just some examples; there are many ways to make your topic visually interesting and engaging for your audience.

Now that you have an idea for what your visual aids will look like and what they'll represent in terms of your talk's content and message, it's time to consider when they will appear during your presentation. You'll want to make sure they complement the style and tone of your talk as well as its focus on specific ideas or points that need emphasis. For example: if one point in your presentation is about how advancements in technology have changed our lives for the better over the last decade, you could use a video clip from a movie that shows someone using a mobile phone or other technology.

If your presentation is about how to improve the environment, you could use photos of people planting trees and other greenery, as well as charts showing how much carbon has been reduced over time. If your talk is about a new education initiative and how it's improving the quality of life for people in a country where poverty is prevalent, you could show photos of children learning and smiling in classrooms.

The key to choosing what visuals to use is making sure they are tied to specific points or ideas within your presentation, and that they will help support those ideas. However, don't feel like you have to cram every idea into one slide; sometimes less is more, especially when it comes to visuals. Be careful not to overcrowd your slides with too many different images or too many words (even if they're short). Remember: Your audience members should be able to focus on one thing at a time without being distracted by other things on the screen — this will help them retain information better and remember what you've said later on.

Warning. In some settings, visual aids and props are inappropriate. Make sure you know what will be expected before you plan to use these elements in your talk.

Should You Script Your Talk?

Preparing an entire presentation can be time-consuming and challenging—especially if you're not used to scripting a speech. Even so, it's certainly worth it for the benefits it offers in return. Here are some things to consider before deciding whether or not to script your entire presentation:

For a presentation to be successful, all its elements must work together to tell one cohesive story. That means every visual and verbal element should support the main message of your talk.

To do this, you may want to consider writing out your entire presentation word for word.

Whether or not you should script your presentation depends on who you are giving it to and what purpose it serves. It's not just about whether or not you can read aloud without stumbling over your words; it's about finding the right balance between being natural and being formulaic.

Benefits of Scripting

When you're looking to give a killer talk, with no interruptions, there's no better way to prepare than to script it from start to finish. Not only will this help you organize your thoughts and ideas, but it will also give you a clear outline for your presentation. This means you can avoid going off on tangents or forgetting important points along the way. If you're someone who tends to get lost in the moment and forget your talk as you move forward, scripting your entire presentation can be a lifesaver.

Scripting is a great way to organize your thoughts

If you're using a script, you can easily skip over any parts that you're not prepared to talk about. Simply do not include such content in your script. This will help you stay on track and give your audience a fully fleshed-out talk without any wasted time or information.

Scripting can help you feel more confident on stage

If you're nervous about being on stage speaking to an audience, nothing will help you feel more confident than having a script in hand. Having an entire speech written out in front of you will help you stay calm and collected throughout your presentation. You'll have a clear outline to follow, and you can use the script as a crutch if you feel yourself getting nervous or anxious. If you're worried that you might forget what you're supposed to say next, you can always glance down at your notes to get you back on track. Having a script on hand will help you feel more natural and confident on stage, even if you're slightly nervous.

When you're prepared and have your talk in writing, it will be so much easier to keep your composure on stage. You'll feel more in control of your thoughts and words.

When it comes to company presentations, more and more professionals are scripting their entire speech. The logic is that rehearsed presentations are less likely to go off-script and risk saying something embarrassing or unprofessional.

Eliminating the potential for awkward pauses also makes it easier to rehearse and cuts down on the number of revisions needed before a presentation. In theory, scripted speeches also make it easy to reuse parts of the presentation again later.

Scripting can help you become a more polished speaker

If you want to be a successful speaker, you need to stand out from the crowd. You need to be memorable and different from every other speaker out there. While you may have some killer ideas and information to share, if you're not a polished speaker, people won't remember you. They might not even make it to the end of the presentation.

By scripting your entire presentation, you're more likely to have something memorable. Your entire speech will be polished and well-organized from beginning to end. It will be a consistent and cohesive message from start to finish. This will help you stand out from the crowd.

Scripting can help you avoid forgetting important points.

Whether you're speaking on a serious or light-hearted topic, it's easy to forget to cover an important point or two. When you're speaking off the cuff, it's easy to lose track of your thoughts, get sidetracked by questions from the audience, and forget to mention something that you really want your audience to know. When you script your entire presentation and know exactly what you want to cover, you won't be likely to forget or overlook any important points. You'll have an outline and checklist of everything you want to say, so there's no way you can forget anything important.

When Should You Script Your Presentation?

So, now that we've covered why scripting your presentation is a good thing, when exactly should you script your presentation? There are certain types of audiences that benefit from a fully scripted talk more than others, but the decision is ultimately up to you. It depends on the type of talk you're giving, the type of audience you're speaking to, and the amount of time you have to prepare. Generally speaking, you should script your presentation if you're giving a formal talk to a large group of people at a conference or business event. You should also script your presentation if you're speaking to a large or non-native-English-speaking audience.

Benefits of Not Scripting

But while there are benefits to scripting your whole speech, not everyone should adopt this practice.

Scripting can backfire if you have trouble reading without sounding awkward. If you want scripting to eliminate practice, it will not. Scripting also limits your ability to follow the audience's reactions and adjust accordingly.

Instead of scripting your entire presentation, you could focus on building trust with your audience and practicing several different approaches beforehand so that nothing catches you off guard.

If you are extremely knowledgeable in your topic and comfortable with your audience, scripting may not be necessary. In this case, having a complete outline of your points could be enough.

Real World Example

I was in a meeting once and was asked to share a few thoughts about the upcoming Christmas holiday season before the meeting ended (no, this was not a company meeting).

Having only twenty minutes to prepare, but knowing I had a friendly audience, I jotted down a few bullet points. It went something like this:

- Mention Christmas and what it means to me – focus on giving and serving others.

- Tell the story about delivering the piano on Christmas Eve.

- Comment that not all service needs to be such a grand gesture.

- Wrap up – how much I like Christmas and how I look forward to it every year.

That was enough to give me about ten minutes' worth of content. Let's break it down, though, to see what I did.

First, I introduced my topic by talking about Christmas and the fact that it's my favorite holiday. It always puts me in the mood for giving. It was maybe two or three sentences. From there, I went straight into a story of a friend helping me to deliver a piano I had bought for my wife for Christmas. He'd kept it in his basement for a month, and we sneaked it into the house around midnight. He was a good friend.

Next, I pointed out that giving gifts or providing service doesn't have to be expensive or grand. It could be something simple.

I concluded by reiterating my opening comment about loving Christmas.

What should you do?

If you're worried about being unprepared for your talk, scripting your entire presentation is a fantastic way to be sure you have all your bases covered.

My general rule is that I script when I will be recording my presentation ahead of time. That way, I can edit out anything I don't like and even redo entire sections if necessary.

I will also script when my talk is oral only, with no formal presentation. I know people who can talk for 30-60 minutes using only notes, but 10-15 minutes is usually my limit.

On the other hand, if I'm using a presentation deck, I try to organize my slides so that each slide tells me exactly what I need to say. We'll talk about using slide decks later.

Practice is Key

If there is one thing that everyone knows about public speaking, it's this: practice makes perfect! It really does pay off in the end if you put in enough time practicing before delivering an actual speech in front of an audience. Even if you do feel confident about what it is you will say during a speech, don't skip out on giving yourself plenty of opportunities to practice your delivery in front of a mirror or video camera. You might not be able to see yourself very well when you are practicing, but it is still extremely important that you develop a good sense of how you will look when you deliver your speech. If possible, try practicing in front of an audience as well so that you can get some feedback on how well your words are being received by the people listening to them.

Don't be afraid to make mistakes during practice either! It is much better for you to learn from the mistakes you make while practicing than it is for you to have those mistakes occur during a real speech because then everyone will know about them. As long as they happen during practice, nobody will even notice, and they won't have any effect on your confidence level or overall performance. By making mistakes and learning from them while practicing, you will be able to avoid making those same mistakes when delivering a live speech and therefore ensure that your presentation goes off without a hitch.

Preparing to Your Deliver Your Talk

You've spent hours practicing your presentation, editing it again and again, and now the moment has arrived. You are about to deliver your talk in front of an audience for the very first time. To help you successfully deliver your talk, there are some strategic considerations that need to be made before you step on the stage:

What should I say? How should I pace myself? What preparation do I need to have? These are just some of the questions you may be asking yourself as you get ready to deliver your talk. If you're feeling anxious or unsure — you're not alone. There is a lot that goes into delivering an effective talk, even if it's your first one! However, this does not mean that you should let these anxieties hold you back from giving your best. Here are my top 10 tips on how to prepare to deliver your talk:

Dress for your audience

In most cases, you won't be expected to wear a suit and tie, but you should be sure to dress professionally. Keep these things in mind: If you're delivering your talk at a convention or a conference, it's a good idea to do some research beforehand to find out what the typical dress code is for that particular industry. If you're giving a talk in a traditional business setting, a business suit is an appropriate choice. Other options include a collared shirt and nice pants, or a collared shirt and nice skirt. If you don't feel like you can make a business suit work for you, then you can always go with a nice blouse or shirt and slacks or a skirt. You may want to consider consulting with a trusted friend or colleague to help you select an outfit that is both appropriate for the occasion and that you feel comfortable in.

Hydration – Drink water, no carbonation or ice

Make sure that you stay hydrated before your talk by drinking a lot of water. Not only does water help you stay hydrated, but it also flushes out toxins and reduces bloat. Avoid carbonated beverages or drinks with ice since they can also cause bloating. Bloating can make you feel puffy and less confident. You may want to bring a couple of water bottles with you to your talk or event so you can sip on them throughout your presentation. You may also want to keep a handkerchief with you to dab the sweat from your brow. If you don't want to bring a handkerchief with you, you can always use the hem of your shirt or dress.

I remember during one presentation, I had a cup of ice water on the table next to me. As is encouraged, I frequently took drinks from the cup throughout the presentation. What I hadn't realized until later was that I was chewing the ice in the cup also! Don't do that. The audience never said anything, which is probably why I never noticed. My boss did, and he gently recommended I ensure that there is no ice in my glass in future presentations.

This goes for carbonation, as well. If you are a soda drinker like I am, you probably know what happens when you drink them. That's right, gas. The urge to belch becomes almost overwhelming, which is not something you want to be doing in the middle of your speech or presentation.

Empty your pockets

Nothing can distract you or your audience more than a bunch of jingling keys or change in your pockets. Make sure you don't have anything in your pockets before you start your talk. You don't want them to fall out and distract you or your audience.

This was my number one weakness for many years. If there was something in my pocket, I would nervously reach in and grab them. Like with the ice, I was entirely unaware I was doing it until a friend pointed it out to me. Now I make sure my pockets are always empty before I begin.

Silence Your Devices

Besides the fact that it is incredibly rude to your audience to be on your phone, social media, or any kind of device during your presentation, do you know how distracting your device's notifications are to you?

You may think you can manage the interruptions, but the truth is, you can't ignore notifications like text messages, emails, and social media posts. Instead, you'll find yourself getting distracted by them and losing your train of thought. If you must have your phone on you during your talk, turn it to silent so you don't get interrupted by notifications. You may also want to turn off all notifications for the duration of your talk, so you don't get distracted by them.

A note on smartwatches

There was a video circulating a while ago showing the President of the United States checking his watch repeatedly during an otherwise somber occasion. It wasn't a good look, and his political opponents lambasted him for it.

After I got a smartwatch myself, I think I understand. It is nearly impossible to resist looking at it when it vibrates, regardless of what else is going on. For this reason alone, I recommend removing it completely. If you don't want to do that, at least set it to "do not disturb" until your presentation is over.

Fresh Batteries for Your Presenter

Do you plan to use clickers or a remote control device during your talk? Make sure you have fresh batteries for it. They are often the difference between a successful talk and a hugely embarrassing one. If you don't have fresh batteries, you could accidentally lose control of your presentation or not be able to turn the lights off if you want to conclude your talk with a dark scene or slide. Avoid risking your talk by making sure your remote control device has fresh batteries.

Rehearse your timings

If you're new to the world of public speaking or you're presenting in front of a large group, it can be easy to go off-schedule. Going well under or over your allotted time is a sign of disrespect to your audience and organizers.

To avoid this, rehearse your timings. When you do, you'll have a better idea of how long you need to spend on each part of your presentation as well as when you need to wrap things up. This will help you stay on track during your actual talk.

If your talk is scripted, you can make notes in the margin indicating how much time should have elapsed by the time you reach that part of the talk.

Preview the Location

Unless you've delivered your talk in this particular location before, you won't know what equipment is available to you or what type of lighting you'll have to work with. If you're not sure what you're working with, take a look at the space ahead of time. This will help you know what type of equipment is available to you and how it will affect your talk, so you can plan accordingly. For example, if you know that there's a window behind you that produces a lot of natural light, you can decide if you want to stand with your back to it or turn off the lights so it's not a distraction.

Decide whether to sit or stand

Some experts believe that standing while you're delivering your talk will make you more energetic and enthusiastic, while others believe that sitting behind a desk or podium will help you appear more confident. If you're comfortable standing, go for it, but if you prefer to sit, that's okay, too. It's about being comfortable so you can focus on being confident and engaging with your audience.

Personally, I tend to slouch when I sit and I don't feel as dynamic. Thus, I prefer to stand, even during virtual calls. On the other hand, I pace when I stand, which does not work at all on camera. Practice doing both and see which position makes you most comfortable.

Know Your Body Language

Your body language will often speak louder than your words, so make sure it's saying what you want it to say. Avoid these common mistakes:

- Don't cross your arms across your chest or place your hands in your pockets (see above about the keys). This is a defensive gesture that doesn't project confidence or authority. Instead, keep your hands open, palms facing towards the audience. This will help you appear more approachable and confident.

- Avoid leaning back in your chair or sitting with your legs wide open. This will make you appear more relaxed, but it could also make you come across as unapproachable or bored. Instead, sit up straight and align your knees with your ankles.

Breathe

Before you start, and occasionally during your talk, take a deep breath and remember why you are standing in front of people

It can be easy to get caught up in your nerves before a talk, so take a moment to focus on your breath. Take a deep breath in through your nose and out through your mouth.

Remember that you are there because you want to share your knowledge and insights with the world. You are there because you love what you do. Keep these things in mind and you'll be sure to deliver your best talk yet!

Delivering Your Talk

Now that you're prepared to deliver your talk, all you have to do is get out there and do it. Remember, there are no mistakes in public speaking, only learnings. As you speak, you will make mistakes, but that's okay — it's all a part of the process. The only way to get better at public speaking is to practice it and get out there, so you can share your knowledge and insights with the world!

Start with a Theme Statement

This is the beginning of the first section of your presentation, "Your Big Idea. It is meant to focus your audience's attention and to help them plan ahead for listening.

A theme statement is a condensed summary of your entire talk. It should let your audience know what you'll be discussing, what they might expect to hear, and why they should care.

The theme statement is one of the most important parts of your presentation. It will help you stay focused while writing and will help you with your presentation delivery.

Of course, your theme statement can be a bit more involved than just a few words. Keep it short for clarity and let your audience know what to expect.

This should be a natural outflow of your takeaways. It's what the audience should remember at the end of your talk.

What you don't want to do is simply state your topic. I'll touch on this later in my section on what not to do.

A good theme statement can save you from a lot of trouble. It makes you appear thoughtful and organized, since you've clearly thought about how best to present your topic. It can also help you to organize your thoughts, since you'll need to condense your entire presentation into a single sentence.

Write a theme statement that is three to five sentences long. The first sentence should include the topic you are discussing and tell your audience what they will learn. The next few sentences should tell your audience the specific insights they can expect to learn. The last sentence should tell them why they should care and how the information you're about to provide will help them.

Stay on topic

Have you ever been listening to someone giving a talk or a presentation and they go off onto this wild, unrelated tangent? I like to call this a "Great Pumpkin monologue" from the Peanuts cartoons. Linus is speaking on a specific topic, and suddenly announces, "But first, a few words on the Great Pumpkin." It's important that you avoid rambling and that you stay on topic.

This can be a challenging for some speakers, who have a fear of silence and feel the need to fill the space with words. They fail to realize that it's better to say few words than many words that don't mean anything.

If you have a tendency to go off on tangents, you need to work on your focus and discipline. If you have a tendency to ramble when you're nervous, it's always a good idea to have a few things ready to say about the subject at hand.

How can you keep from rambling? Turn off your inner critic and relax. If you scripted your talk, consider marking your place as you proceed through it.

Speak slowly, clearly, and loudly

It is important to speak clearly and slowly so that your audience can understand what you are saying, and because rushing through your talk can give your audience the impression you are unsure of yourself.

Be careful not to mumble. Many people when speaking in public get nervous. This is natural. When that happens, they often start speaking too quickly and sometimes mumble. When you feel yourself starting to get nervous, pause at the end of a paragraph, take a deep breath, and restart the next paragraph slowly and clearly.

Another common mistake is to speak too softly. You do not want to shout but should be loud enough that people can hear you anywhere in the room.

Make sure you are projecting to the back of the room by standing up straight, putting your shoulders back and your head up.

Some people have trouble speaking loudly even when they know they should.

The more nervous you are, the louder you should speak. And the more important the occasion, the louder you should speak.

Practice before your speech, making sure that you have the volume you need. One way to be sure you are using a suitable level of volume is to record yourself speaking a few paragraphs in the back of the room before your talk. Play it back to see how it sounds and adjust your volume accordingly. It's best to have a partner help with this if you can.

Try to avoid disfluencies like "like" or "um". These are filler words that usually indicate that you are searching for the next thought in your mind. This can be hard, but if you slow down and take your time, you should be able to eliminate most of these.

If you are using a PA system, try to position the microphone to be approximately 10-12 inches from your mouth. Speak up but let those conducting the meeting worry about the volume.

The awkward pause

This is one of my personal quirks. Sometimes I will simply forget my next word. Usually, it takes the form of a forgotten conclusion to a point I'm trying to make. It goes something like this:

"And if you do this well, you'll quickly see that..." and then nothing.

I have learned to overcome this by making sure that conclusion statement is somewhere on my slides (if I'm presenting that way). At other times, when I find myself in an awkward pause, I'll quickly shift gears and ask the audience what they think. Something like this:

"And if you do this well, you'll quickly see that... well, what do you think the outcome will be?"

That usually works, though I caution again about using that strategy more than once or twice in a given talk.

Make eye contact

It's important to make a connection with your audience. You do that by making eye contact with them. As you begin to speak, look around the room and try to pick out a friendly face (or 5). As you deliver your talk, try to move your eyes between your paper or presentation and those people you've chosen.

Talk to your listeners. This is a simple concept that is easy to overlook. Instead of talking to the horizon, look at the people sitting in front of you. Use visual cues like waving your hands around to indicate stuff happening in the next slides. It is easier to speak to the people sitting in front of you than to a screen.

An alternative to this strategy is to look at the back of the room, just above the heads of those in the very back. To most people in the audience, this will appear that you are making eye contact with those behind them. It is not as desirable but may help if you have a hard time finding enough friendly faces.

Be careful when asking for audience feedback

A common mistake many public speakers make is to ask too many questions that require the audience to respond, either physically (raised hands) or verbally.

As I mentioned previously, I will ask for feedback when I'm stuck, but that's a coping mechanism I have developed for a particular situation. It isn't something I plan, and recommend the same for you.

In a classroom or professional setting, asking the audience to raise their hands is acceptable. For example, asking the listeners who is familiar with the topic is common. Asking a second question is sometimes called for as a follow-up, but three times in a single talk is overkill, and audiences do not care for it. After two or three times, many people in your audience will simply stop responding.

Do not ask the audience to look up definitions

This is a delaying tactic. Many speakers who do not have enough material will ask listeners to look something up, answer questions, or otherwise provide feedback during their talk.

This takes the pressure off the speaker, but it also allows the audience to stop paying attention for the duration of whatever process the speaker asks them to do.

If you really want your audience to look something up, include a link in your presentation. If you are worried that listeners will be dissatisfied with the amount of material you provide, then you need to provide more material.

Do not use long, irrelevant quotes with no additional analysis

Using relevant quotes can add a lot of power and authority to your talk. Some people make the mistake of using really long quotes, and never bridge the gap with their audiences as to its relevance.

This is a surefire way of losing your audience's attention.

Before deciding to include a particular quote in your talk or presentation, ask yourself:

- Is this directly relevant to the point you're making?

- Is it short enough that it won't distract from the main point of your talk?

- Is it a quote or is it really a story?

If it's a quote, you'll want to make sure you attribute it properly.

It isn't enough to quote someone; you must tie it back to your topic. Make sure you add a paragraph or two, or a sentence or two, that explains why that information is useful and important to your topic.

The key to using a quote is not simply to repeat it, but to extrapolate the quote and apply it to your own ideas. Also, be sure to add your own analysis of the quote. This will make your talk more immediate and engaging to the audience.

Tell relevant stories

Humans are story-telling creatures. Everyone loves a good story, whether it's delivered on paper, in a movie, a TV show, or verbally. The best talks use a lot of stories to get their points across to their audiences.

Make sure, however, that you do not use stories that are not pertinent to your topic.

Consider starting your talk with a story related to your topic. this will pull your audience into your talk emotionally, and effectively communicate your topic.

Avoid overused stories

Many stories have been told so many times, that they are almost cliché. People are tired of hearing them. Rather than bolster your talk, telling an oft-told story could cause people to tune out.

That's not good.

Some stories are so familiar, just hearing the beginning of them will bring you the rest of that story.

Some examples are:

- Footprints in the Sand

- The Boy Who Cried "Wolf"

- Alice meeting the Cheshire Cat in Alice in Wonderland

- The boy and the starfish on the beach

If you've told a story and people in the audience seem not to have heard it before, you may be okay to tell it. Or you may want to consider finding a new story or twist to bring to it.

The best stories are the ones directly from your life and experience. They are uniquely your stories, and you can be pretty sure no one has ever heard them before.

You've got stories from your life. Share them.

Finish in the time assigned

As I mentioned earlier, this is simple courtesy. If you are assigned to give a 10-minute talk, taking longer cuts into the time of the speakers following you. Likewise, going shorter leaves extra time that someone else may have to fill.

The other speakers on the program have worked hard to prepare and deserve the time they signed on for.

It's good form to go a little under time, rather than over. For example, say you have 10 minutes, but your topic will take only 8 minutes. If you finish in 5, it's not a big deal, but if you end in 3 (or even less), this is likely to make the next speaker feel rushed.

Practice your talk

You never know how your talk will sound, or how long it will take, until you've practiced. Practice delivering your talk aloud, and time yourself. If you can, deliver it to someone you can trust and who will give you honest and constructive feedback.

If you can, record yourself and watch it after a brief delay. You will certainly find things you can improve. You will probably find that you fidget, talk too fast, or too softly.

Practicing your talk will only make you better.

Wrapping Up

Restate Your Topic

Up to this point, if you've done your job well, everyone knows what the topic was. Now is the time to be explicit about it. This would be a good time to read your theme statement.

Summarize Your Talk

People learn through repetition. You've probably made several pertinent points throughout your talk. Summarize them bullet-point style.

PowerPoint Tips

Though I have tried to make my tips in this book apply both to talks, speeches, and presentations with and without slides, I don't think it would be complete without adding some tips for using PowerPoint (and other slide deck software) effectively.

What's the most important thing in a presentation? Of course, it's the slide. But with so many slide formats, themes, and tricks available, how do you know which one is best for your audience? Before you start your next presentation, keep these slide presentation tips in mind to succeed.

Don't read your slides

Ideally, they won't contain much text to be read. They will have text, but that text should be minimal and simply help to keep you on track.

The ideal slide has fewer words and more pictures. Talk to your audience and don't make them read.

What if you are giving a detailed business proposal? You may be required to share the presentation with customers. If the presentation doesn't have text, it could be impossible for them to understand the presentation.

If you are building a deck for both presentation and handouts, consider putting text on every other slide and hiding those slides during the public presentation. When you create the handouts, include them.

Use more pictures, fewer words

Pictures are worth a thousand words, right? A lot of the time that's true. It's more difficult for your audience to read a bunch of text on a slide and retain any information. That's why it's important to include pictures in your slides. Another thing to consider is how many words you should have on each slide. Ideally, you should only have three bullet points per slide. Having too many words on one slide will make it difficult for people to take in any information or remember what you said once they leave the presentation. If you have more than three points, break them up into separate slides and put links at the bottom of each page so people can click through if they want more details.

A great story I heard once was about a live presentation that had no words (except the intro screen, so the audience knew they were in the right room). Pics from unsplash or pexels can make a complete presentation. Granted, this takes a lot of practice, but the effect can be amazing.

Use a Professional Design

I'm not a designer. As a result, my advice to others like me is, "don't act like you are." Provide little text, but make it very legible, add pictures, but make them relevant and/or entertaining.

If you want your slides to look clean and professional, it's best to use simple layouts. This will keep the attention on your slides and what you have to say. This also ensures that viewers can quickly skim through your presentation for the important points.

Tip: If you can manage it, get a designer to help make your slides look great.

Bonus Tip: Newer versions of Microsoft PowerPoint contain AI-generated slide designs. Most of them are pretty good.

Pay attention to color and contrast

Contrast is largely what determines how clear a slide is to your audience. The most important thing you need to pay attention to when making your slides is the contrast between text and background. If you have a light-colored text on a dark background, it can be hard for people to read. Conversely, if you have dark-colored text on a light background, it can be difficult for the reader's eyes to adjust from the background once they enter the slide.

In general, black and white are ideal because they offer high contrast levels. Text in any color other than black or white may not be as visible against its background. This doesn't mean you should use only black and white as these colors can appear harsh to some viewers. However, if you want your presentation to be successful, create it with contrast in mind.

PowerPoint is about conveying info, not becoming the next Picasso. Simple themes are best. How will your presentation look with the lights turned off? With bright lights on?

Animations and transitions

You don't need a lot of animations; they're a pain to set up and they're mostly a distraction. Unless the animation itself has to communication a specific kind of meeting, at best, you need a fade in.

Avoid gaudy transitions beyond simple fade-in/out.

Font sizes

The best way to get your message across is with a large, bold font. You want the text to be easy on the eyes and big enough for everyone to read, with caveat of not having too much text. This will help them stay focused on what you're saying during the presentation. If you have bulleted points or other important information, make sure they stand out.

Use Slide Sections

You can name your slide sections. DO THAT. That should be your speaking outline

Use Notes

Don't use the slide to tell you what to say. That's what the "notes" section is for.

Wrap up with a takeaway

The last slide of your presentation should be a summary of what your audience can take away. Ideally, you want everyone to agree (without really knowing anything about the content) that they've learned something valuable and that this was worth their time.

Your takeaway slide could include some key points or major points from the presentation. This will help ensure people don't walk out with nothing in mind, or worse, walk out without remembering anything at all.

Things to Avoid (Analyzing the "Worst Talk")

Remember that "worst talk" from the beginning of the book? In this appendix, I want to go through it again and discuss why it was so bad, beyond the obvious.

For context, I wrote this talk with the intention of breaking as many of my rules as possible.

The text of the talk is in *italics* and my commentary is not. Some of the commentary is identical to what I included previously in the book but presented again alongside the example.

So, let's start.

Audience Interaction

Good morning, folks. [If no one responds, repeat it until you get a response.]

There are a few problems with this opening. First, it is somewhat informal. In most professional settings, even in the classroom, you should err on the side of being more formal or professional.

Second, most talks are not interactive. Depending on your audience, sometimes you will get a response to a greeting and sometimes you will not. It is not necessary (or even desirable) to try to elicit responses.

There are times to get audience feedback or participation, but usually only if you need information to decide which direction your talk should take. For example, you may want to ask for a show of hands to see if you need to cover a basic topic. Your audience will likely let you get away with two such questions, possibly three, before they simply stop responding. So, you want to use this sparingly.

Introducing Yourself

For those of you who don't know me, my name is Michael Callaghan and have been in this company for the past ten years.

I recommend you do not introduce yourself at the beginning of your talk. Why?

If you introduce yourself, you are taking time away from the very the reason everyone is there.

I see this mistake being done at conferences, as well as user group meetings. The presenter takes it upon themselves to formally introduce themselves, their company, and what their talk is about. I prefer to get right into the subject of my talk, without any formalities. The formalities are usually covered in the welcome letter sent out to the attendees before the event.

The audience doesn't need to hear it again.

Most likely, you have already been introduced by the person conducting, and there is no reason to do it again. It only wastes time.

Also, introductions are not very interesting.

This is what the attendees expect: great content.

Exception: It is possible, however, that you were not already introduced. In that case, and you think your audience may not know who you are, feel free to offer a brief introduction. Don't go into a long biography. Try to stick to your name, occupation. Add company and job title, if appropriate.

Occasionally, you may be asked to share a brief biography about yourself or your profession. In such a situation, it is certainly appropriate to do so. This will probably be the exception.

Humor

Today I intend for my talk to be like a ghostly elevator – it will lift your spirits! [Chuckle at your own horrible joke]

Opening a talk with a joke is nearly a cliché. Everyone seems to do it. My advice is to be careful.

Humor is a tricky thing to get right, especially for novice speakers, and in many settings it may not be proper. Too many things can go wrong. At best, you get a great reaction. At worst, you could end up offending someone in your audience. The most likely scenario is that you get a polite response.

Unless you are certain your joke is both funny and right for the situation, you may want to drop the humor.

If you insist on using humor in your talk, make sure you rehearse your delivery and timing with someone who will give you honest feedback.

Never use self-deprecating humor at the beginning of the presentation. Self-deprecating humor is when you make fun of yourself by saying something along the lines of, "I'm a klutz. I tripped pulling into the parking lot. I'm very clumsy. I fall down a lot..."

Unless you are the most hilarious and entertaining speaker I've ever heard, this will not work. You will lose your audience's attention.

Announcing Your Topic

My manager asked me to speak for a few minutes on the state of software development at our company.

Analyze almost any talk or presentation and you will find that the speaker rarely announces the topic ahead of time. Follow that example and let your content do it for you.

Use your opening paragraph to provide the topic without resorting to an explicit statement. I will expand on this idea later.

Also, if the meeting was very well planned, the attendees know that the purpose of the meeting is a presentation by the person they know and have come to see.

The details of the talk is another matter.

Questioning Your Selection

I don't know why she thought I was the right person to speak about this. I spent most of the week trying to get out of it, but I didn't do a very good job, so here I am.

Probably everyone who has ever spoken in front an audience has internally questioned their fitness for the assigned topic. It is also called "impostor syndrome" and we have all experienced it.

However, explicitly questioning during your talk sets up an expectation of failure in your listeners. Instead, prepare your talk to ensure that the things you say are true and relevant.

Some things to keep in mind:

1. Choose topics you are qualified to speak about. Don't be afraid to say 'no' if you do not feel comfortable. This is not to say you should only speak about things you are an expert at, but you should be prepared to explain the bits you are less familiar with.

2. Know your material inside out.

3. Don't show the speaker notes during your talk.

Complaining About the Talk

I hate speaking in public, even to small groups, so I put this off till this morning.

One of the worst things you can do in your talk is tell your audience you do not want to be talking to them. It is completely unprofessional and counterproductive.

Further, complaining about giving the talk is a lousy way to start. It sets the wrong tone and tells everyone in the audience that you don't want to be there, and probably didn't prepare well.

Even giving a single talk is a big undertaking and should be treated as such. If you are planning to give a talk, you should feel honored to be invited or volunteering to speak.

If you are not excited about giving your talk, then don't do it. If you feel you do not want to give your talk, then do not give your talk.

Even if you say, "I'm going to be giving you a talk I'd rather not give," somehow that comes across as condescending.

Take responsibility for the fact that you are there, that you volunteered to speak. And while you may be nervous, you'll be fine.

What if you didn't and you really don't want to be there but have no other choice? Hopefully the tips in this book will let you get through it intact. Who knows? Maybe you'll find that you enjoy it after all.

Apologizing Ahead of Time

I apologize in advance for this talk's poor quality. I was too bogged down with my important work to prepare.

Have you ever been to a talk where the speaker apologizes for not being as prepared as they want to be? Or they come up with what they hope are amusing reasons that the talk will not be interesting.

Maybe they did not have enough time or know the material well.

Don't do this. You are setting yourself up to fail. Most people in your audience will never notice whether you've prepared adequately.

People understand you are nervous and will usually give you the benefit of the doubt. They understand that talks can be uncomfortable and will empathize with you. They will forgive your mistakes and imperfections. Announcing them ahead of time is setting yourself up to fail.

False Gratitude

Even so, I am grateful for the opportunity for me to get up to speak to you today. Talks are supposed to be a great opportunity for y'all to learn from me, but I definitely learned more writing it.

While it is true that you will probably learn your topic more deeply by preparing for a talk, you need not mention it. I have heard people say this often that enough that it seems to be a common trope, which you are better off avoiding entirely.

More importantly, you are already speaking in public. If you were not prepared to do so, you would not be presenting. The fact that you are giving a talk about something you know well implies that you have spent a lot of time thinking about and working with the material.

Definitions

According to Wikipedia, the definition of software development is "the process of conceiving, specifying, designing, programming, documenting, testing, and bug fixing involved in creating and maintaining applications, frameworks, or other software components.", which is far better than the definition at dictionary.com. That site doesn't even attempt to define it.

Do not start with a dictionary definition of your topic. This is the mark of an ill-prepared speaker, and it feels lazy.

Your best opening is to deliver a brief personal story, directly related to the topic, that will help set the tone.

If you have delivered a well-received talk in the past on the same or a similar topic, it's OK to use the same story to help establish rapport with your audience.

The story should be about two minutes long. You can make it longer, but if it goes on for more than three minutes, people begin to get restless.

Irrelevant Tangents

To me, software development is a lot like those old Peanuts cartoons. For example, consider the Great Pumpkin. Linus proclaimed that "Halloween will soon be with us, and on Halloween night, the Great Pumpkin rises out of the pumpkin patch, and brings toys to all the good little children." The other characters in the cartoon react to Linus the same way many people in my family react when I talk about software.

I love stories, analogies, and metaphors in a talk. They can really draw the audience closer to you, especially when the topic is related to your story. In this case, the connection is weak, and feels like a distracting tangent.

The former US President Bill Clinton was famous for beginning speeches with a story that had nothing to do with the topic of the speech but established his relationship with his audience.

I recently heard about a book author who began his talk with a short story about teaching his five-year-old daughter to ride a bicycle. It had nothing to do with the topic of his talk.

So, some people may be able to pull it off, but I recommend staying on topic.

Overused and/or Irrelevant Stories

I would like to share with you a story I heard at a conference once. Most of you are familiar with Alice in Lewis Carroll's classic novel <u>Alice's Adventures in Wonderland</u>. You will remember that she comes to a crossroads with two paths before her, each stretching onward but in opposite directions. As she contemplates which way to turn, she is confronted by the Cheshire Cat, of whom Alice asks, "Which path shall I follow?" The cat answers, "That depends where you want to go. If you do not know where you want to go, it doesn't matter which path you take." That, my friends, is how I feel some of our software projects go.

Likewise, here is another story which does not relate well to the topic. Minor diversions and tangents can sometimes strengthen a talk, but to be effective, you need to be able to tie them together.

Whenever you provide a story, make sure it supports your topic. It may be necessary to explain how it does so. If the explanation is no longer or more complex than the story itself, you are probably safe.

If you need to add a lot of explanation, then you are not doing a good job of presenting the story.

If you have a number of supporting stories, you will want to pick them such that they are coherent, that they illustrate your main points, and are relatively independent of each other. A series of stories which are too inter-dependent will detract from each other.

We have all heard a speaker who used a story to prove a point. It contributed to the development of the talk, but the story did not provide any insight into the topic. It was obvious that the speaker had not spent enough time to think of a story to relate to the topic.

Don't be that speaker.

Weak Conclusion

In conclusion, I'd like to thank you for coming.

A good conclusion should summarize the information presented in a concise way, reminding your audience about the key points of your talk.

The conclusion above does not accomplish that in any way. The conclusion is thoughtless.

It feels like the writer is just trying to get through the task of finishing the talk.

The conclusion should state the main problem or point and then suggest an action to solve it.

The conclusion is often a good place to restate your main points, but be sure to do it in a more general way. By doing this, you can remind your audience of the main points and conclude your presentation.

The second is a minor irritation of mine. Do not tell your audience that you would "like to" thank them.

A Simple Request

I hope you enjoyed this book. If I have offered even one piece of advice you find helpful, then I consider the effort of writing it as time well spent.

Please consider leaving me a positive review at the store where you purchased it. Also consider some of my other titles you find there.

Do you have any advice about giving talks from your own experience? Share them with me. Feel free to email me with questions, stories, or comments at michael@walkingriver.com. Who knows? Your story might make it into my next book!

You can also sign up for my email list and check out my other content offerings at https://walkingriver.gumroad.com.

Please follow me at Twitter for regular updates. My handle is @walkingriver[1].

---

1. https://twitter.com/walkingriver

Don't miss out!

Visit the website below and you can sign up to receive emails whenever Michael D Callaghan publishes a new book. There's no charge and no obligation.

https://books2read.com/r/B-A-FCXP-OXNKD

BOOKS 2 READ

Connecting independent readers to independent writers.

Also by Michael D Callaghan

Angular Advocate
Developing Progressive Web Applications with Angular: How to Build and Deploy Mobile Applications without Paying Apple or Google for the Privilege

P-AI-R Programming
P-AI-R Programming: How AI Tools Like GitHub Copilot and ChatGPT Can Radically Transform Your Development Workflow
Pair Programming with Chat GPT

Standalone
Don't Say That at Work
Customizing ChatGPT: Quickly and Easily Create and Share Custom Business-Specific GPTs Without Code
How to Deploy Any Web Application to the Apple App Store
Sacrament Talk Mastery: How to Give a Sacrament Talk When You Really Don't Want To
The Scout Law of Leadership: 12 Attributes Every Leader (or Aspiring Leader) Should Cultivate
Techno Tales

¡No Digas Eso en el Trabajo! Lecciones que Puedes Usar para Mejorar tus Habilidades de Comunicación en los Negocios
How to Give a Talk When You Don't Really Want To: Tips and Techniques to Improve Your Public Speaking

Watch for more at https://walkingriver.com.

About the Author

I began learning to program computers way back in 1981 in High School. The Data Processing teacher took pity on a young 9th grader and let me borrow time on the county's HP 2000 to teach myself BASIC. That experience grew into a passion for software development that has never waned.

Though my early career took a 10-year detour, I finally began writing software professionally in 1995. I've been doing that ever since.

Read more at https://walkingriver.com.